THE CORPS OF DISCOVERY

The GREAT EXPEDITION of LEWIS AND CLARK

By Private Reubin Field,
MEMBER OF THE CORPS OF DISCOVERY

As recorded by JUDITH EDWARDS

Pictures by SALLY WERN COMPORT

Farrar Straus Giroux / New York

To Benjamin, Will, Carolyn, Martha, and Aaron
–J.E.

To Allan, my partner in all discoveries
–S.W.C.

Text copyright © 2003 by Judith Edwards
Illustrations copyright © 2003 by Sally Wern Comport
Distributed in Canada by Douglas & McIntyre Ltd.
Color separations by Phoenix Color Corporation
Printed in the United States of America by Phoenix Color Corporation
Designed by Nancy Goldenberg
First edition, 2003
1 3 5 7 9 10 8 6 4 2

Library of Congress Cataloging-in-Publication Data

Edwards, Judith, 1940–

The great expedition of Lewis and Clark : by Private Reubin Field, member of the Corps of Discovery / as recorded by Judith Edwards ; pictures by Sally Wern Comport.

p. cm.

Summary: An account, told in the words of one participant, of the difficulties and wonders that were part of the Lewis and Clark expedition to explore the land obtained as part of the Louisiana Purchase.

Includes bibliographical references.

ISBN: 0-374-38039-2

1. Lewis and Clark Expedition (1804–1806)—Juvenile literature. 2. Field, Reubin, ca. 1771–1822?—Journeys—West (U.S.)—Juvenile literature. 3. West (U.S.)—Discovery and exploration—Juvenile literature. 4. West (U.S.)—Description and travel—Juvenile literature. [1. Lewis and Clark Expedition (1804–1806). 2. Field, Reubin, ca. 1771–1822?—Journeys. 3. West (U.S.)—Discovery and exploration—Juvenile literature.] I. Comport, Sally Wern, ill. II. Title.

F592.7 .E38 2003
917.804'2—dc21

2001059756

My name is Reubin Field. Private Reubin Field. My brother Joseph and I just started farming our 640 acres of land here in Jefferson County, Kentucky. Once in a while, as we're tending our fields and livestock, or fishing in the Ohio River, we imagine we're still paddling on the great Missouri. Big Muddy, that river's called more often. You can bet we know why for sure, better than anybody in the world— except for maybe thirty or so other men and one Indian woman who were also part of the Corps of Discovery.

Not everybody believes the tales we have to tell about our 863-day adventure. For starters, there was the time we were camped out on a sandbar in ole Big Muddy. We slept mid-river that night to get away from the mosquitoes and gnats that swarmed all over us and tried to camp out in our noses and eyelids. The mosquitoes had been so troublesome that day, even the dog was yelping.

We were sound asleep when all of a sudden Joe woke up and screeched like a hoot owl. That sandbar was sinking right out from under us, with Big Muddy sneaking into our boots. Did we move fast!

Or the time a buffalo came stampeding through the campground. Seaman, Captain Lewis's dog, saved us that time. He set out a-barking and scared that curly buffalo so bad, he turned and bolted out of camp, his hoof one inch from my head.

So what were a bunch of grown men doing putting up with mud, mosquitoes, and midnight visits from large wild animals?

You can blame President Thomas Jefferson. He decided he needed to explore the new territory the United States government bought in 1803 from Emperor Napoleon in France. The Louisiana Purchase, they called it—828,000 square miles of land west of the Allegheny Mountains. Got a good deal too: bought the whole thing for just fifteen million dollars.

President Jefferson had a few things in mind about this exploration. He wanted to know about the different tribes of Indians who lived out West, mostly so we could trade with them for valuable furs. He wanted to know about plants and animals and the climate and geography. But he especially wanted to know if a boat could travel all the way from Missouri to the Pacific Ocean. A northwest passage. He found out!

That's where we came in. Jefferson chose Meriwether Lewis to be Captain of this expedition. Captain Lewis chose his good friend William Clark to be Captain with him. Then the Captains had to find a bunch of strong young men like Joe and me to become the Corps of Discovery.

Captain Clark put the word out along the frontier, up the Ohio River in Indiana Territory, that he wanted able woodsmen and hunters for a long trip up the Missouri. The reward, if and when we got home, was a piece of land. Adventure plus a farm when we got back? That's all Joe and I had to hear. Captain Clark thought we were strong-built and able, and he chose both of us. The Field brothers headed for St. Louis!

The catch was that we had to become soldiers first. This was a military expedition and we had to learn RULES. It wouldn't do to get out in some forest with a group of hostile Indians and not be able to obey the kind of orders that could save your life.

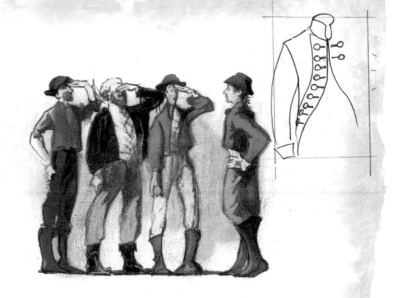

So we marched and we drilled and we got up before dawn and went to bed with the chickens—unless we could get by with sneaking off for a little fun. A couple of the new soldiers, including me, had a *real* hard time with the discipline. Even John Colter, the best hunter and scout anybody could want, got confined to camp for going off without permission and having himself too good a time in town.

You'll never hear me say one bad thing about Captain Lewis or Captain Clark. The two bravest, fairest men in the world, those two. Worked just as hard and went through all the dangers we did without a word of complaint. And that first winter, when we were camped out in Woods River, Illinois, across the Big Muddy from St. Louis, they worked hard at getting us to work hard, that's for sure.

By the time spring came and the boats and supplies were ready for us to head out, we were a special unit of the army. Then we packed everything into the keelboat, which looked like a big wooden box and could double as a fort if we ran into hostile Indians, and we headed upriver.

May 14, 1804. Off we sailed! Well, not exactly. Upriver meant just that—against the current. Most of the time we were standing up to our waists in mud. Pushing. Or standing on the crumbly, sandy riverbanks, pulling that hunk-o'-wood keelboat along with ropes. Snakes slithered around our legs, and oh, those mosquitoes!

When we met our first group of Indians, from the Oto and Missouri tribes, they laughed at us. Our uniforms—what was left of them—were muddy and bedraggled, and here we were pulling an ungainly wooden box. The Captains put on a grand show to impress them. Captain Clark shot off a noisy air gun. Captain Lewis read a long speech about the Indians' Great Father Jefferson back in Washington, and gave them a bunch of medals and trinkets.

We were invited to a feast in their village, and our boatman, Pierre Cruzatte, played his fiddle for dancing. Big York, a slave who was Captain Clark's servant, was a source of great fascination. The Oto and Missouri Indians had seen lots of white men before, but no black men. They thought he was painted. York growled and acted fierce and we all had a grand old time.

All except Moses Reed, the coward. He was always grumbling, especially about those troublesome mosquitoes. So he just up and deserted. When the Captains caught up with him, he was made to run the gauntlet. That was the last discipline problem we had on the whole trip.

At one point George Shannon, just seventeen, got lost. Even John Colter couldn't find him. We were just pulling out to go upriver when a sorry-looking creature appeared on the riverbank. He'd been lost for sixteen days and survived on one rabbit and a bunch of wild grapes!

The saddest thing was when Charlie Floyd, one of the sergeants, got a terrible stomachache that didn't get any better. He died right on the banks of the Missouri. We buried him and made a cross for his grave.

Then we proceeded on—which was what we were always doing. We met some other friendly Indians, the Yankton Sioux, who warned us that the Teton Sioux upriver weren't so friendly. In fact, as we found out, they were downright ornery. Did *they* ever laugh at us! No speeches or medals would win over those Indians.

Captain Clark and a few of us paddled over from the keelboat and brought their chiefs back for a visit. That went all right, but when we delivered them to shore again, a couple of Indians on the bank grabbed hold of the towrope on Captain Clark's canoe. The second chief, called the Partisan, pushed Captain Clark, who got real red in the face. Captain Lewis ordered the guns aimed from the keelboat. Thirty Sioux warriors aimed bows and arrows. Everybody shouted.

The grand chief, Black Buffalo, assessed the situation and told the men holding the towrope to let go. I hate to think what could have happened to us and the whole expedition if we'd all started fighting.

The next day these same
people acted like we were their best
friends. They sat the Captains up on buffalo robes
and carried them into their village. Big celebration, as usual. Things seemed fine until
a captive Indian from another tribe told us there were plans to kill each and every
one of us the next morning! We were up and out of there before dawn, with a whole
bunch of angry Teton Sioux howling and running along the riverbank after us.

It was getting on for winter, already October. We had a good stay with the Arikara
Indians and then went on to some Mandan villages. The Mandan helped us find a
place to build a fort for the winter. In those far northern parts, winter means forty
degrees below zero, with snow up to your eyeballs.

We went out hunting for
buffalo with the Mandan. It was
a little embarrassing how they
outrode us, their men killing
twice as many buffalo as us
"tough" wilderness explorers.
We got some meat to put by
for the winter, though.
When we began to run out
and winter just kept freezing
on, we traded tools for
the Mandan's corn.

That same winter, a Frenchman, Toussaint Charbonneau, who'd been working as a trader with the Hidatsa Indians, had come trudging into the fort. Behind him were a couple of his Indian wives. One of them, named Sacagawea, was pregnant. She was only about sixteen years old. Turned out she'd been captured from her Shoshone tribe by the Hidatsa as a little girl, and then old Charbonneau bought her from them. Charbonneau could speak French and Hidatsa, and Sacagawea spoke Hidatsa and Shoshone. Charbonneau liked the idea of being paid, I guess, so he wanted to sign on as an interpreter. While the Captains were deciding about Charbonneau, they let his family stay in the fort.

Poor Sacagawea! She sure had a hard time giving birth. René Jessaume, another interpreter who'd been living as a trader with the Mandan for fifteen years, told Captain Lewis to give her a potion made from the rattle of a rattlesnake. Seemed to do the trick, because tiny little Jean Baptiste Charbonneau yowled his way into the world, and into our hearts, that very night.

So, when we left Fort Mandan that spring of 1805 for unknown territory, little Pomp, as he came to be called, and his ma and pa came right along with us. And that wooden tub, our keelboat, was sent back to St. Louis with plants and animals we'd collected to show President Jefferson the new things we'd found. One of them was a prairie dog. We sure had a time catching him.

Moses Reed went too, along with the regular soldiers. Then it was just us, the Corps of Discovery: thirty-one grown—or almost grown—men, one woman, and one baby. We had six small canoes, and two larger ones called pirogues. This was the whole fleet. Captain Lewis said that our ships might not be quite as respectable as those of Columbus, but they sure gave these adventurers pleasure. And here we were, heading off into what was, for us, unknown wild country that was at least two thousand miles wide.

We could have done without certain unwelcome company that showed up from time to time. That uncivilized grizzly bear! I still wake up at night dreaming I'm scurrying up a tree to get away from the fellow.

Nothing we could do about it, though. We had to kill a bear now and then, just to keep clothed. You should have seen us. We'd given up on our raggedy uniforms at the fort. We had to sew our own clothing out of animal skins. And there was no more wearing boots; we wore moccasins, just like Indians. We were so dark-tanned from the sun, if it wasn't for the fact that we had beards, which the Indians didn't wear, you couldn't have told we *weren't* Indians.

Meat was our staple food, and that meant hunting every day. We could go through a whole buffalo or five elk in one meal. Sacagawea found root vegetables underneath the soil, like the Shoshone ate, which gave us some variety. Sacagawea was calm and steady. Nothing ever got her upset. But that husband of hers, Toussaint, wasn't much good to us except when he was interpreting.

I'll never forget the day one of the pirogues hit a big swell and started careening from side to side. Charbonneau was at the rudder, and he started shrieking and hollering. He only calmed down when Pierre Cruzatte threatened to shoot him if he didn't take hold of the rudder.

All kinds of stuff fell overboard, and there was a lot of flailing around. Sacagawea didn't say a word, just waded into the river with her baby on her back and began picking things up.

That was just before we came to the forks, each one wide and deep. This created a problem. Which way was the Missouri?

All of us men thought we should take the north fork. Only Captain Lewis and Captain Clark thought we should go south. We trusted so much in the Captains' good judgment that we said we'd go whatever way they said, even if we thought differently.

Do you think they were right?

Well, of course they were! We proceeded upriver, hoping to find a waterfall the Mandan had told us about. They said we'd have to get out of the canoes and portage them for about half a day before getting back on the water.

Then—what a noise we heard one day! Around a bend was a *gigantic* falls eighty feet high and three hundred yards wide. When we walked along the bank we found four more, almost as big.

We camped along the river and the Captains started planning. This would be no half-day portage. We built two wooden carts that we'd drag back and forth across the riverbanks with the canoes and the supplies. The ground was rutted and sharp from buffalo hooves. Prickly-pear cactus spines poked through our moccasins, and we had to repair them every night and make new ones every two days. The mosquitoes even attacked our eyes. Storms with lightning and thunder struck suddenly and hard.

When we stopped to rest, I was so tired I fell asleep on the way to the ground. At least we weren't hungry; the hunting was good, with elk, antelope, and buffalo all around.

Finally we had carted the canoes and supplies past the last falls. We continued upriver to an area that looked as if the cliffs were opening a gate for us. Captain Lewis called this part of the river the Gates of the Rocky Mountains.

Then the river became narrow, and the bottom was stony and shallow. We were constantly using poles to push and towlines to pull. The river was running out—coming near to its source. It was time for us to find the Shoshone and cache our canoes. We needed horses to climb that little mountain-way before coming to the next river.

I can still hear Sacagawea's laughing voice telling us we were going to be all right. One bright summer day she pointed to a large rock she said was called Beaver's Head. She knew we were near the three forks of the river where she had been captured as a little girl by the Hidatsa. The summer living quarters of the Shoshone had to be nearby.

Captain Lewis took me, Private Hugh McNeal, and George Drouillard, one of our interpreters and scouts, with him on foot across the hilly land. Captain Lewis was out ahead and the rest of us walked spread out behind him. We carried our rifles in our arms, which were folded across our chest. We needed to be cautious but not look threatening; these Shoshone had never before seen a white man.

And there he was. A lone man, silhouetted against the summer sky.

Captain Lewis stopped and waved his blanket as a sign of friendship. He pulled his sleeve back to show the white skin beneath his shirt.

I don't know why we didn't have the sense to stop advancing, or at least lower our guns. Captain Lewis sure was angry at us later, especially at me, because I was the last to stop. That Indian just turned his horse right around and galloped off.

We had to set up camp and try again the next day. McNeal stood with one foot on each side of this tiny stream coming right out of the ground. Captain Lewis said we'd reached the farthest fountain sending water to the mighty Missouri.

A few days later our luck turned. We came across three Indian women. They sat with their heads bowed down, probably afraid we would kill them. They stopped being frightened when we gave them some presents. Figuring we were friendly, they led us into the Shoshone village!

The Shoshone were suspicious of us at first, but when a few of them came to our main camp at the three forks and saw Sacagawea and Pomp, they knew we must be peaceable. No Indian ever went on a war party with women and children.

Here's the part that's really hard to believe. When Sacagawea went into Chief Cameahwait's lodge to interpret for the captains, they were mighty surprised to see her burst into tears. She ran over and threw her blanket across Cameahwait's shoulder. Turns out he was her brother! That's called a coincidence—and the honest truth.

The Shoshone were real good to us, and sold us all the horses we needed to cross the fierce Bitterroot Mountains. Still, it was late August, and we were worried we wouldn't get over those mountains before winter set in.

On Lolo Pass, all the difficulties we'd had before seemed easy by comparison. The horses lost their footing and started sliding down the steep mountainsides, sending our supplies skittering with the rocks. There was no game to hunt. We boiled our candles and killed young horses for food. We named one campsite Hungry Creek because we didn't have anything to eat that night.

Then came the snow, and it fell fast and deep. We were weak and sick. A few of us who could still walk went with Captain Clark to see if we could find an Indian camp. What must the Nez Perce have thought when this bedraggled group of white men staggered into their village? Had they been hostile, they could have killed all of us right then and there, without much trouble.

Instead, once again, at the end of a truly awful mountain crossing, Indians saved our lives. The Nez Perce helped bring the rest of the group into their village, and we stayed with them, getting stronger, for two weeks. They showed us how to burn out the inside of a tree to hasten the building of a dugout canoe.

We launched these vessels down the Clearwater River, bound for the Columbia River and the Pacific Ocean. Up by that ridge, called the Continental Divide, where Captain Lewis saw the mountains that nearly did us in, the way the water flows changes directions. Now we were speeding downriver, the current pushing *us*.

We fairly hurtled down the Clearwater and cascaded onto the Columbia. We paddled the canoes over the rough water and the many little falls. Lots of Indians watched us from the banks.

3 feet Decent
3 feet 6 inches decent
6 feet decent
rapid of 3 feet decent
9 half a feet decent
cascades of 13 feet

These Northwest Indians were different from any other tribes we'd met so far. The Chinook Indians had had their heads flattened between two boards when they were babies, which they considered a sign of beauty! They weren't so companionable, either. European traders had been coming off boats on the Pacific for some years, and the Chinook drove a hard bargain when we wanted to trade for food. But we were going fast along this wide river, through rapids and fog, and so glad to be doing it.

I'll never forget the day Captain Clark shouted, "Ocean in view! O, the joy!" You can imagine how happy we were. It turned out to be only a large bay, and it took us a few more days to reach the real Pacific Ocean. Great waves and shimmering water meeting up with the sky—and no mountains in the way. We yowled and hollered and ran along the shore.

Then, while looking for a site to set up camp, we got marooned by fog and rain for three weeks at Cape Disappointment. Terrible weather! It was time to find a place for the winter. Of all the fair things the Captains did on this expedition, how they chose a location for our fort was the fairest. They took a vote of the whole company, including York and Sacagawea. We chose a cove the Clatsop Indians told us about, near the ocean but safe against storms. There we built our last winter encampment: Fort Clatsop.

It wasn't a very exciting winter, that's for sure. We had a lot of work to do—clothing to repair, new moccasins to sew. And we had to rig up a bunch of boiling kettles to make salt from ocean water. Ever tried to swallow dried, boiled elk meat without any salt? That was our New Year's Day dinner, January 1, 1806.

We had, by Captain Clark's reckoning, traveled 4,162 miles. He worked on a map of the country we'd crossed, and Captain Lewis wrote in his journal about all the amazing new plants and animals we'd seen. Animals such as bighorn sheep, grizzly bears, antelope, mule deer, jackrabbits, badgers . . . I could go on. Captain Lewis tallied that we'd seen, all new to us, thirty-three species of mammals, thirty species of land birds, and twenty-six species of waterbirds.

And we added another marvel to that list the day we spotted a whale beached near the fort. That meant oil to cook our food and make that elk meat taste a mite better. We made plans to take a party off to the ocean to cut up the whale.

And here's where Sacagawea spoke up for the first time in the whole journey. She let it be known, without any doubt, that she was not happy about being left behind. Here she'd traveled all this long way with us to see the great waters, and now we weren't going to let her see them *or* the great big fish. Well, Captain Lewis made sure Sacagawea went along to see the whale!

Finally it was time to take
our salt, our new moccasins,
and ourselves back home. We
were almost out of trade goods,
but we had gunpowder and
plenty of ink and paper so the
Captains could write about
the journey and make us all
famous.

We were rowing against the current again, and the Chinook Indians were always trying to steal things from us. Three Indians even tried to steal Seaman! But we chased them, and when they saw our angry faces, they let him go.

Before we reached the Nez Perce village, we stayed with the Walla Walla Indians. Captain Lewis knew a lot about medicine; he set broken bones and treated fevers and the eye problems that plagued the Walla Walla because they watched the sunlit waters so many hours to spear salmon. Chief Yellept traded a beautiful white horse for Captain Clark's sword and some ammunition.

Next we had a good reunion with the Nez Perce, and this time we weren't weak and sickly. Their braves competed with us in all kinds of games. Sometimes we even won! This passed the time while we waited for the snow in the Bitterroots to melt.

I don't blame the Captains for starting out too early; they were just as impatient as we were to get home. The snow was so deep we lost our way and had to turn back— the first time ever during the whole expedition. The snow finally melted and we proceeded on again.

When we reached the end of the Lolo Pass, we broke into two parties so we could explore the country around both the Marias and Yellowstone Rivers.

I went with Captain Lewis to explore the Marias River and try to make contact with other Indian tribes. We made that contact—and nearly lost our lives.

The Blackfoot Indians controlled the country around there. They were just as fierce as their cousins, the Teton Sioux, and didn't like the idea of white men taking over their fur trading.

Eight of these fellows came up on us one day all friendly-like. We smoked the peace pipe. That was our first mistake.

We camped together that night. Our second mistake.

I woke up near dawn to hear George Drouillard shouting. He was struggling with an Indian who'd grabbed his rifle. Another man grabbed Joe's rifle, and I got out my knife and went after him. I'd just stabbed the Indian in the stomach when Captain Lewis grabbed the stolen weapon and shot an Indian who was running away—with the Captain's rifle!

Two Blackfeet were dead and the others were escaping after trying to run off with our horses. We caught them and mounted up. It was time to ride hard and fast before the warriors called out the whole tribe against us. We rode day and night for 126 miles. Our canoes were where we'd left them, and we jumped in and sped down the Marias River. Safe!

While we were busy almost getting ourselves killed, Captain Clark was exploring the Yellowstone River with the rest of the men and Sacagawea. With her help, he mapped many passes that would make it easier for people to travel in the western lands in the future. Captain Clark even etched his name on a big rock he named Pompy's Tower, in honor of little Pomp, who was now almost a year and a half old.

Wm Clark
July 25th 1806

The current was at our backs, and we zoomed down Big Muddy. At the Mandan villages, the Charbonneau family left us, though Captain Clark promised he'd take little Pomp and educate him as if he were his own son when he got a little older.

Would you believe, after all these dangerous months–*years*–that John Colter decided to ask leave to go back upriver to trap beaver? The Captains just thanked him and wished him well.

Somebody made a joke about seeing buffalo along the banks when we spotted our first cows. We knew we were almost home.

High noon, September 23, 1806. Five thousand people waved from the riverbank as our little fleet reached St. Louis. They'd given us up for lost, we'd been gone so long. Two years and four months! After all that time, everyone alive and well except poor Charlie Floyd. Home at last.

Well, it's back to work for Joe and me tilling our very own ground, all peaceful and calm. Telling the tales that seem too strange to be true, stories about a wild and beautiful land that'll never be quite so wild again. I wonder what will happen in the years ahead to all of that vast, open land? Will people move out to the Louisiana Territory, some of them to farm just like we do? Will more men like John Colter go out there just to hunt and trap? Riding over the mountains, fighting the surging rivers . . . just like we did . . .

What do *you* think?

Who Was Reubin Field?

Reubin Field was born in Culpeper County, Virginia, around 1771 and moved with his family to a two-hundred-acre farm on Pond Creek, in Jefferson County, Kentucky, in 1790. He and his brother Joseph were two of the "nine young men from Kentucky" recruited by William Clark in 1803 for the Corps of Discovery. Reubin was a good hunter, and was with Lewis during the most exciting and dangerous events of the journey.

After the expedition, Reubin bought the Pond Creek farm from his parents for $500. In 1807 William Clark petitioned the Secretary of War to raise Reubin's rank to lieutenant, but the request was refused. In 1808 Reubin married, sold the Pond Creek farm, and moved to Indiana. He returned to Kentucky in 1816, buying another fifty acres on the Little Bee Lick. Reubin Field probably died in 1822.